LEARNING ROOTS

HAJJ and UMRAH Activity Book

This book belongs to

....

NOTES FOR GROWN-UPS

Who Is This Book Suitable for?

This book contains activities for 5-7 year olds.

Your Feedback is MORE Than Welcome!

Every effort has been made to ensure the information contained in this pack is accurate, authentic and pedagogically sound. If you find anything to the contrary, we welcome your feedback at: **www.learningroots.com/feedback**

Stickers, Cut-Out & Pull-Out pages

In order to make learning fun and varied, some of the activities in this book require the use of stickers, cut-out objects and pull-out pages. All of these sections are clearly labelled in the book and are referenced on the contents pages. Please ensure you supervise your child when cutting objects from the cut-out pages, or have an adult cut it for them. Similarly, please keep the stickers out of reach from small children under the age of 3 years.

Suggestions on How to Use this Book

We highly recommend that you **be present to support your child** while they do the activities, in order to foster, create and cherish quality faith-filled moments with your child.

Sharing or Copying Pages from this Book

For the best experience, this publication has been designed to be used by one child. If you would like to use this book with more than one child, such as a large household or a class of children at an educational institution, please purchase one book for every child. Please contact us at **support@learningroots.com** for details on our discounts for educational institutions. Otherwise, no part of this publication may be reproduced, stored in a retrieval system, or transmitted, in any form, or by any means, electronic, mechanical, photocopying, recording or otherwise without prior written permission from Learning Roots.

Some activities require a **grown-up** to help explain or read instructions.

Simple reference numbers for you to find your way.

Four categories cover the main topics in Hajj.

Key skills are used to develop your child holistically.

Some activities make use of **stickers** which you can find at the back of the book.

CONTENTS

Off we go!

TRAVEL JOY

Meet the Families

● With the help of a (grown-up), dress each child in the families correctly by matching the descriptions of their clothes to the (stickers) provided. You'll meet the team in the activities to come!

Thabit

A white thobe.

Aisha

A pink dress with yellow trim.

Daddy

Zayd

A white top.

Sofia

A spotty dress.

Uncle

Sarah

A pink dress with a purple cardigan.

Layth

A stripy shirt.

Mum

Dad

Hiba

A striped dress.

Granddad

Qays

A blue top.

TRAVEL JOY

Your Very-Own Passport!

● With the help of a **grown-up**, follow the steps below to create your very own passport! You'll be collecting stamps in your passport during your journey.

1 With the help of a **grown-up**, use scissors to cut out your passport from the cut-out section at the back of this book.

2 Fold the passport in the middle, as shown above.

3 Fill in the information on the first page to make this passport personal to you!

4 At each stage in this book, you'll add **stickers** to your passport, showing the places you have visited.

FINE MOTOR SKILLS

PREPARE

Let's get ready for Hajj by learning about its history and virtues!

Get a **Hajj & Umrah Visa** stamp on your passport from the stickers section. See Activity Number 2.

Hajj to the House

Allah told the Prophet Ibrahim ﷺ to build a special place where people from all around the world would come to pray to Allah alone.

This was a very important job, so Ibrahim ﷺ asked his young son, Ismail ﷺ, to help. Both father and son got to work in the middle of the hot Arabian desert and started to build the Kabah beside a well called Zam-Zam.

Ismail ﷺ went out looking for the best stones and brought

them to his father. Ibrahim ﷺ stacked the stones one on top of the other and built a strong wall. There was just one problem.

As the walls got taller, Ibrahim ﷺ could not reach high enough to stack more stones on top. That's when something amazing happened.

Allah sent the Angel Jibreel with a special stone from Jannah. It was like an automatic lift that Ibrahim stood on and used to reach the top of the Kabah.

When the building was finished, there was one place left empty for a very special stone. Allah sent the Angel Jibreel again with a special Black Stone from Jannah. Ibrahim ﷺ placed it on the corner of the Kabah. Now the first house of worship was complete.

Allah ordered Ibrahim ﷺ to call, people from all around the world to come and visit the Kabah.

There was no-one around when Ibrahim ﷺ made the call but Allah made it reach everywhere.

Today, lots and lots of people from all over the world visit the Kabah on a journey called Hajj.

Hajj is a special journey that every Muslim who is well and able should make. When on Hajj, Muslims get closer to Allah by answering the call of Ibrahim ﷺ.

There are lots of things to do in Hajj, many of which only occur on this special journey. Thankfully, the Prophet Muhammad ﷺ showed us how to do them perfectly.

We are going to learn all about Hajj in this book.

Perfect Pillars

● Discover the five pillars of Islam by matching each **sticker** to its image pair. Use the colours to help you.

Shahadah

Prayer

Zakah

Charity

Fasting

Hajj

Which pillar will you be learning about in this book?

You'll love this one!

PEACE OF HEART

Valuable Virtues

● Match the virtues of Dhul-Hijjah with their pictures, using the **stickers** provided. Use the shape of each sticker to help you.

Your Bad Deeds are Forgiven

Jannah is Your Reward

Your Duas are Answered

You are Allah's Guest

10 Glorious Days

● Trace over the dots to reveal the month and dates of the best ten days of the year.

ذو الحجة

١٢٣٤٥٦٧٨٩١٠

Dhul-Hijjah

1 2 3 4 5 6 7 8 9 10

The Prophet ﷺ said:

"*No good deeds are better than what is done in these first ten days of Dhul-Hijjah.* (Bukhari)"

Hadeeth

PEACE OF HEART

Good Deeds

● With the help of a (grown-up), match each of the good actions illustrated below with its correct description.

○ **Reciting Quran**

○ **Visiting the Sick**

○ **Praying**

○ **Going for Hajj**

○ **Speaking the Truth**

○ **Giving Charity**

Reciting Quran ○

Visiting the Sick ○

Praying ○

○ **Going for Hajj**

○ **Speaking the Truth**

○ **Giving Charity**

Being Good to Parents ○

Visiting the Sick ○

Praying ○

SACRED RITES

When is Hajj?

● Put the Islamic months in order by aligning the **stickers** to make full dots. Then, name the month Zayd is pointing at to discover the month of Hajj.

Muharram

Safar

Rabi'ul Awwal

TRAVEL JOY

Just Enough

Thabit is saving his money to go on Hajj. He needs five gold coins. Does he have enough?

Look for these ones!

TRAVEL JOY

I'm travelling from here...

Use the **stickers** to match each Muslim character to the part of the world he or she is travelling to Hajj from. Use the monuments in their hands to help.

TRAVEL JOY

Packed Out

● Zayd is packing his suitcase for Hajj, using a picture he had taken from his last travel. Help him spot the five differences between his old suitcase and the one he is packing now.

Can you find my Quran and passport?

PEACE OF HEART

Well-Mannered

● Qays is helping his granddad move around in his wheelchair. Spot the five differences between the pictures below.

Helping others is a great deed!

Found it!

- Help Thabit find some of the places and events he will see whilst performing Hajj and Umrah.

U	U	C	B	C	G	J	A	Q	P
D	G	W	C	G	M	N	R	E	H
Z	N	X	D	M	I	N	A	B	Z
S	S	H	M	T	K	K	F	I	I
G	U	M	R	A	H	M	A	T	W
V	Z	P	F	Q	D	L	H	V	Y
H	V	Z	N	I	K	I	M	G	G
A	C	S	J	M	T	Q	N	E	M
J	U	Q	X	D	S	H	E	A	Q
J	M	L	I	H	R	A	M	X	H

1 HAJJ

2 UMRAH

3 MINA

4 ARAFAH

5 MADINAH

6 IHRAM

7 MIQAT

UMRAH

Let's get ready for Umrah. Think of it like a 'Mini-Hajj'.

Get the **Miqat** and **Makkah** stamps on your passport from the stickers section. See Activity Number 2.

SACRED RITES

Umrah Order

● With the help of a grown-up, read the descriptions below and circle the number under each picture to show the order of the actions of Umrah.

1 2 3 4

After tawaf, walk between two mountains seven times.

1 2 3 4

Finally, cut your hair and come out of Ihram.

1 2 3 4

First, wear your special Ihram clothes.

1 2 3 4

Then, go around the Kabah seven times while remembering Allah. This is called 'tawaf'.

Ihram Limits

● Follow the lines of each image to discover what Layth can and cannot do when in *Ihram*.

Not in Ihram

In Ihram

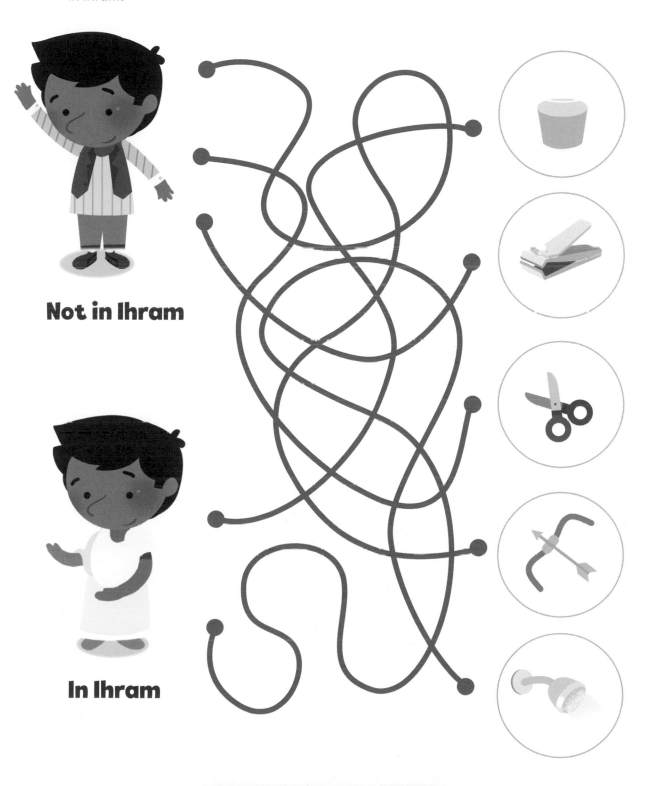

Simple Dress

- Using the **stickers** provided, dress Qays appropriately, ready for when he enters the state of Ihram.

Answering the Call

● Count how many times you can spot the word *'Labbayk'* in the Talbiyyah below.

لَبَّيْكَ ٱللَّهُمَّ لَبَّيْكَ، لَبَّيْكَ لَا

شَرِيكَ لَكَ لَبَّيْكَ، إِنَّ ٱلْحَمْدَ

وَٱلنِّعْمَةَ لَكَ وَٱلْمُلْكَ

لَا شَرِيكَ لَكَ

Answer ....

GOLDEN AGES

The Black Stone

● Fill in the blanks by using the **stickers** as you learn about the history of the Black Stone. Use the pictures to help you match the correct places.

The _____ is from Jannah. It was sent down with the Angel Jibreel at the time when Ibrahim ﷺ was building the _____ . Allah ordered Ibrahim ﷺ to place the stone at the corner of the Kabah.

The Prophet _____ said, "The Black Stone came down from Jannah and was whiter than _____ , then it became black by the bad deeds of people." At the time of the Prophet ﷺ, the stone was really _____ , but today, only a few _____ are left. The Black Stone marks the beginning and the end point of the Tawaf. That's when you go around the Kabah _____ times while remembering Allah.

Around the Kabah

Use the **stickers** to show the characters performing different acts of worship around the Kabah.

Who has finished tawaf and is praying behind Maqam Ibrahim?

FINE MOTOR SKILLS

The Story of Sa'ee

Ibrahim ﷺ left his wife Hajar and their new born son, Ismail ﷺ, in the middle of a hot, dry desert. "Why are you leaving us here? Is it because Allah has asked you to?" asked Hajar.

"Yes," replied Ibrahim ﷺ.

"Then He will take care of us." said Hajar. It was lonely and hot in the desert, and the bag of dates and water that Ibrahim ﷺ had left soon ran out.

Baby Ismail ﷺ started to cry out of hunger. Hajar knew she had to look for help. She climbed up a nearby mountain named Safa. She looked far and wide but couldn't see anything, except another mountain nearby.

So she ran down, reached the other peak and looked far and wide, but she could not see anything, except her baby crying in the distance.

She ran between the two mountains again and again looking for help, until the seventh time, she saw something amazing. It was an angel, striking its heel on the ground, causing water to spring from it.

She came rushing down and gathered the water for Ismail ﷺ to drink. Allah saved Hajar and Ismail ﷺ with the miracle of the Zamzam well.

Blessed Water

● Name each drink, and tick the picture that shows Zamzam water.

SACRED RITES

Sa'ee Sayings

● Move your pencil along the path between Mount Safa and Marwa while saying words of remembrance at the same time. See the box for some suggested words.

Say

سُبْحَانَ اللّٰهِ
وَالحَمْدُ لِلّٰهِ
وَاللّٰهُ أَكْبَرُ

Fantastic
work!

SACRED RITES

Nice Trim

Use the **stickers** to show how each character looked before they came out of *Ihram* and had their hair shaved.

Take your time!

SACRED RITES

Tawaf Turns

● Follow the dots to help Thabit complete his Tawaf by going around the Kabah seven times.

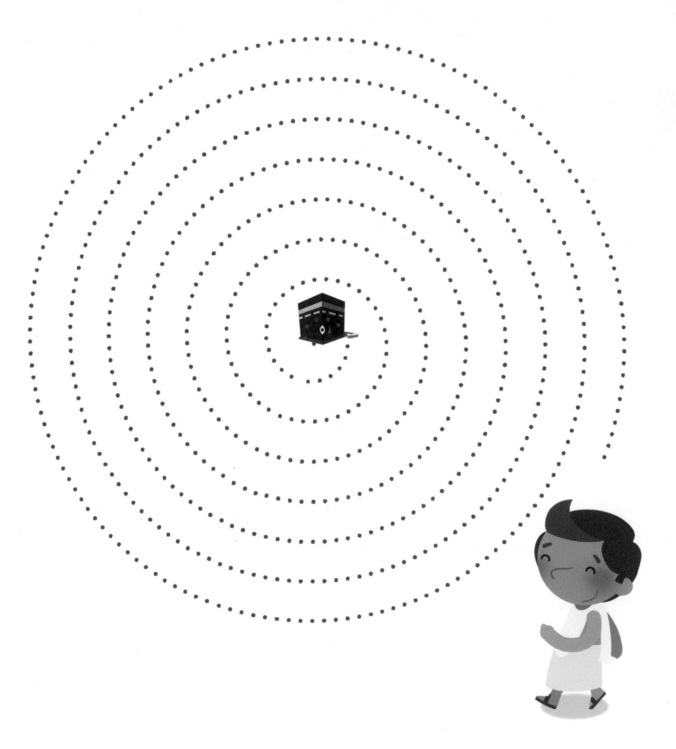

HAJJ

It's time for the great days! You'll remember your Hajj for life!

Get the **Arafah, Mina, Muzdalifah** and **Jamarat** stamps on your passport from the stickers section. See Activity Number 2.

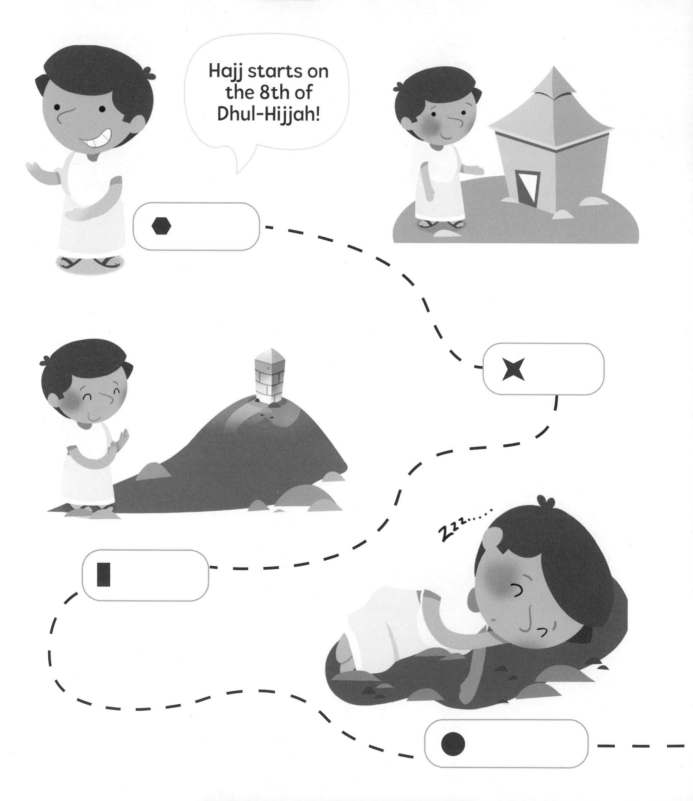

Days of Hajj

● Label the events of Hajj using **stickers**. Use the shapes on each label to help you.

Hajj starts on the 8th of Dhul-Hijjah!

SACRED RITES

Counting Pebbles

● The characters are in Muzdalifah collecting pebbles. Count and add up the pebbles to find out who has collected the most so far.

Sara

$5 + 2 + 8 =$ ....

Thabit

$7 + 1 + 9 =$ ....

Aisha

$4 + 3 + 6 =$ ....

Outstanding effort!

On Target

- It's time to stone the Jamarat. Drop a pencil on the page. Can you strike the Jamarat pillar?

There are three Jamarat towers, and this is the biggest one.

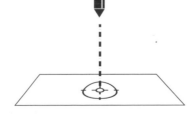

FINE MOTOR SKILLS

The Story of Jamarat

Ibrahim ﷺ saw a dream. In it, Allah (SWT) had ordered him to sacrifice his young son, Ismail ﷺ. Ibrahim ﷺ loved his son so much and even though it was such a hard thing to do, Ibrahim ﷺ decided to do what Allah had asked of him.

"Do what you have been told to do, Daddy." said Ismail ﷺ. "I will be very patient, insha-Allah."

Shaytaan wasn't very happy with this, so he whispered to Ibrahim ﷺ and tried to stop him from doing what Allah said. Ibrahim ﷺ then picked up some stones and threw them at Shaytan until he ran away, but Shaytan didn't give up. He whispered to Ibrahim ﷺ again and again and tried to stop him from sacrificing Ismail 𐏓. Each time Ibrahim 𐏓 pelted him with stones.

Ibrahim 𐏓 made up his mind to follow Allah's command. He laid Ismail 𐏓 down and just as he was about to sacrifice his son, he heard a voice telling him he has passed his test.

There was no need to sacrifice Ismail 𐏓, Allah wanted Ibrahim 𐏓 to show how strong his faith was. Ismail 𐏓 was safe and Allah gifted Ibrahim 𐏓 a large sheep for Ibrahim 𐏓 to sacrifice instead.

Eid Takbeer

What part of Layth's dress is a different colour in each image? Match the speech bubble **stickers** to the colour of this part to find out the order of the Eid Takbeer.

Seven Shares

- The sacrifice of a cow can be shared by seven families. Use the seven **stickers** to complete the picture of the cow.

What sound does a cow make?

FINE MOTOR SKILLS

Eid Fun and Games

● Play these fun puzzle and matching games on Eid by following the steps below:

1 With the help of a **grown-up** cut out the puzzle.

2 Put the pieces together to make the puzzle!

A With the help of a **grown-up**, cut out the squares of the matching game and place them upside down.

Visit your family and friends on Eid!

B Take turns with a partner to turn over two squares. If the two sqaures match, keep them. The person with the most pairs at the end, wins!

1 With the help of a **grown-up**, cut out the Eid cards from the cut-out section and fold them in the middle.

2 If you wish, you can mount the cut-outs on card before filling them in and giving them to your family and friends on Eid!

Eid Stickers

We've added some extra stickers outside of the orange frames in the stickers section for you to use as decorations on cards, envelopes or gifts on Eid day. Enjoy!

The Learning Roots team wishes you an accepted Hajj and a blessed Eid!

Days of Tashreeq

After the 10th of Dhul-Hijjah, the families remain in Mina and stone all the Jamarat pillars for 3 more days. Can you find the characters shown below?

SACRED RITES

Make Your Hajj Scene

Make your very own Hajj scene by following the steps below:

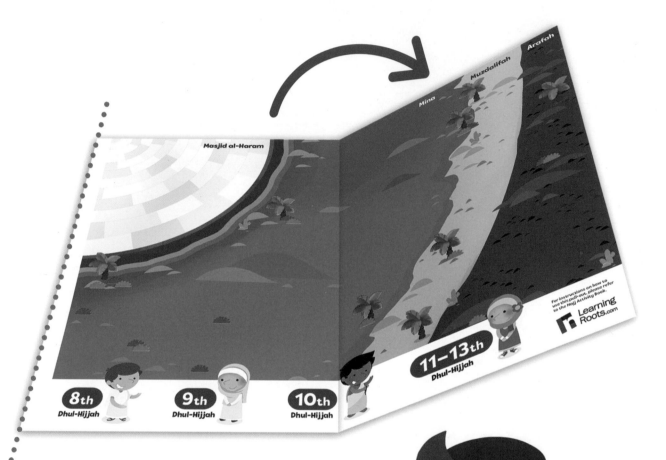

Masjid al-Haram

Mina

Muzdalifah

Arafah

8th
Dhul-Hijjah

9th
Dhul-Hijjah

10th
Dhul-Hijjah

11–13th
Dhul-Hijjah

For instructions on how to use this pull-out, please refer to the Hajj Activity Book.

LearningRoots.com

1 Find the fold-out Hajj scene at the back of this book and very carefully tear it off on the perforated line.

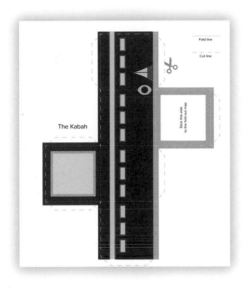

2 Find the Kabah cut-out for the Hajj scene activity in the **Cut-out Section** at the back of this book.

3 Find the stickers for the Hajj scene activity in the **Stickers Section** at the back of this book.

www.learningroots.com/crafts

See Hajj Scene Instructions

4 With the help of a **grown-up**, go online to the following website **www.LearningRoots.com/crafts** to see the instructions on how to make your exciting Hajj scene.

SACRED RITES

Lost in Tent City

Qays is lost in Mina. Connect the dots to find out where he is.

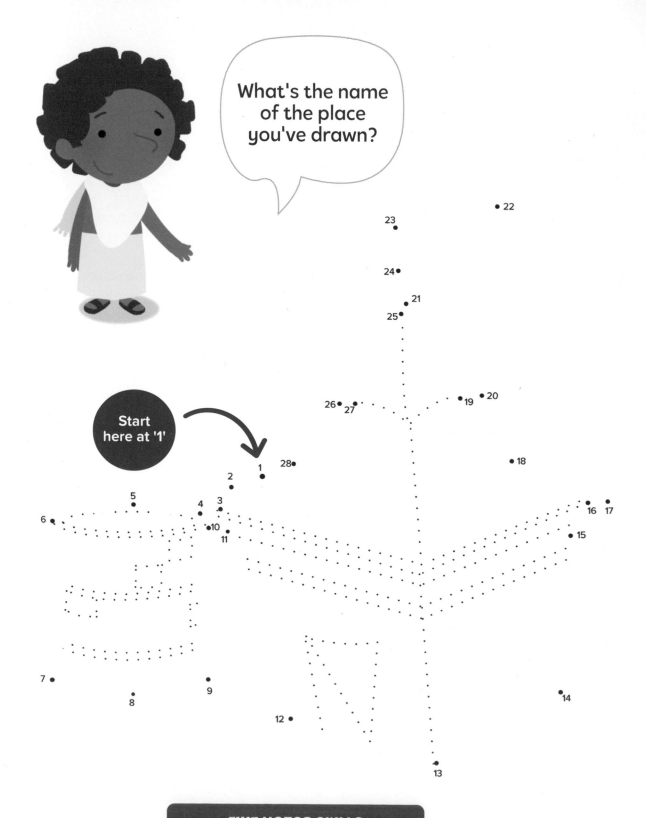

I see you!

What's the name of the place you've drawn?

Start here at '1'

MADINAH

Visit the city of
the Prophet ﷺ.

Get the **Madinah** stamp
on your passport from
the stickers section.
See Activity Number 2.

That's a nice banner!

PEACE OF HEART

Saluting the Beloved

● Use the **stickers** to complete the jigsaw of the name of the Prophet Muhammad ﷺ and then decorate the page with the help of stickers.

What do you say after hearing the Prophet's ﷺ name?

CREATIVITY

PEACE OF HEART

Piece of Paradise

● Using the **stickers**, match the parts of the Prophet's ﷺ masjid to their silhouettes. Discover the special rowdah area by covering the empty space in the middle with the green carpet.

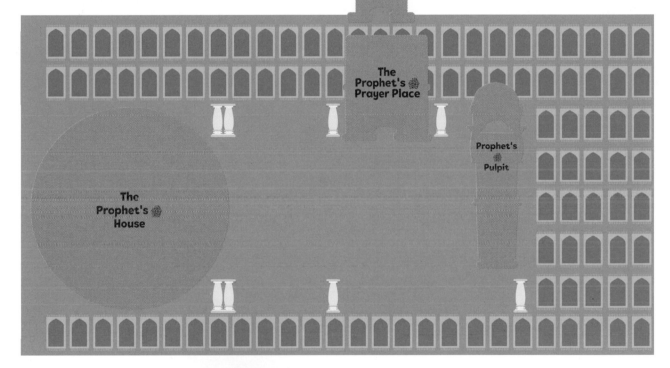

Today's Mihrab

The Prophet's ﷺ Prayer Place

Prophet's ﷺ Pulpit

The Prophet's ﷺ House

The green carpet area is known as 'rowdah' and is a piece of Jannah!

FINE MOTOR SKILLS

May Allah bless you!

PEACE OF HEART

Madinah's Dome

- Follow the steps to draw the dome and minaret of Masjid An-Nabawi.

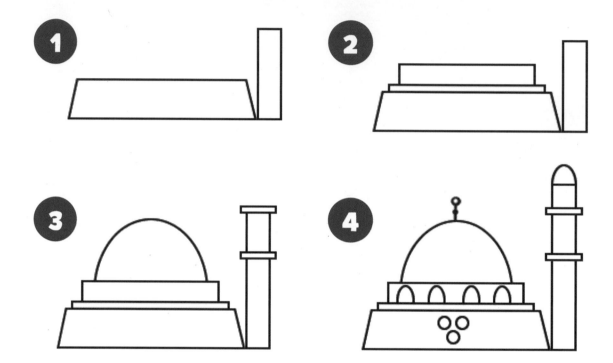

CREATIVITY

PEACE OF HEART

Madinah's First Masjid

● Colour in this picture of Masjid Al-Quba.

This was the first masjid built by the Prophet ﷺ in Madinah!

CREATIVITY

You'll love this one!

TRAVEL JOY

Diverse Dates

- Using the **stickers**, match the dates to the correct piles.

Ajwa

Safawi

Khudri

Sukkari

FINE MOTOR SKILLS

ANSWERS

To see the answers
to the activities in this book,
please visit:

LearningRoots.com/answers

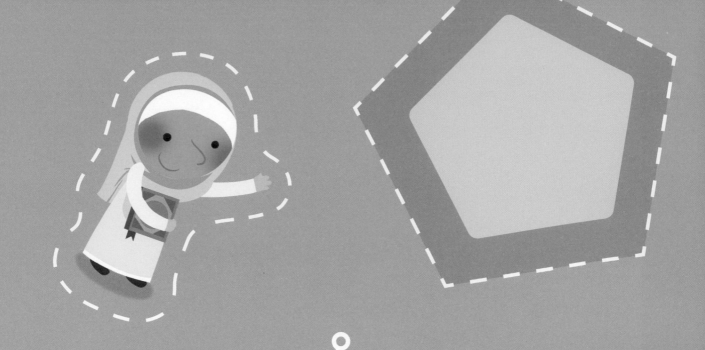

CUT-OUT SECTION

my Hajj

PASSPORT

LEARNING ROOTS

⇆ Passport Name and Details ⇆

Name ....

Age ....

Country ....

Signature

Photo

Cut out the cards, turn them over and mix them up. Then with a friend, take it in turns to find matching pairs of Hajj events and places! Who will find the most pictures?

Learning Roots
Cut-Out Activity

Learning Roots
Cut-Out Activity

Learning Roots
Cut-Out Activity

Learning Roots
Cut-Out Activity

Learning Roots
Cut-Out Activity

Learning Roots
Cut-Out Activity

Learning Roots
Cut-Out Activity

Learning Roots
Cut-Out Activity

Learning Roots
Cut-Out Activity

Learning Roots
Cut-Out Activity

Learning Roots
Cut-Out Activity

Learning Roots
Cut-Out Activity

Learning Roots
Cut-Out Activity

Learning Roots
Cut-Out Activity

Learning Roots
Cut-Out Activity

Learning Roots
Cut-Out Activity

Learning Roots
Cut-Out Activity

Learning Roots
Cut-Out Activity

Make this puzzle using the pieces you've cut out.

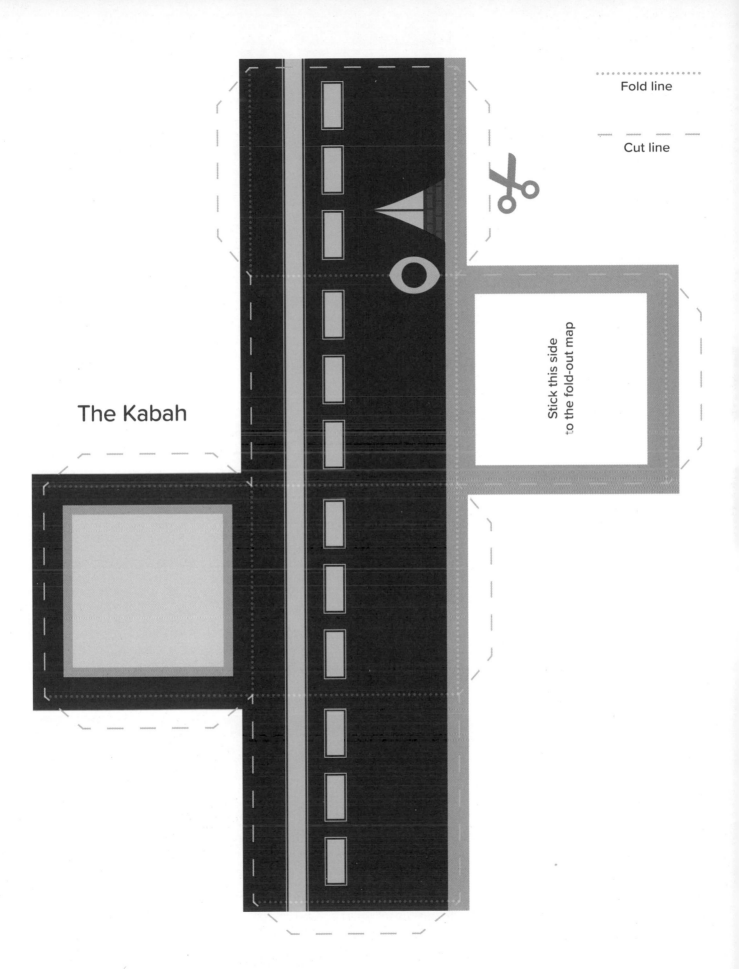

Fold line

Cut line

The Kabah

Stick this side to the fold-out map

Learning Roots
Cut-Out Activity

Learning Roots
Cut-Out Activity

Learning Roots
Cut-Out Activity

Learning Roots
Cut-Out Activity

Learning Roots
Cut-Out Activity

Learning Roots
Cut-Out Activity

Learning Roots
Cut-Out Activity

Learning Roots
Cut-Out Activity

Learning Roots
Cut-Out Activity

Learning Roots
Cut-Out Activity

Learning Roots
Cut-Out Activity

Learning Roots
Cut-Out Activity

Learning Roots
Cut-Out Activity

Learning Roots
Cut-Out Activity

Learning Roots
Cut-Out Activity

Learning Roots
Cut-Out Activity

Learning Roots
Cut-Out Activity

Learning Roots
Cut-Out Activity

Learning Roots
Cut-Out Activity

Learning Roots
Cut-Out Activity

Learning Roots
Cut-Out Activity

LEARNING ROOTS

LEARNING ROOTS

Wishing you a blessed Eid!

Wishing you an accepted Hajj!

STICKERS SECTION

FEEDBACK PLEASE!

We would love to hear your thoughts on this book. Please let us know at:

LearningRoots.com/Feedback

STICKERS

Activity 1

Activity 10

Activity 16

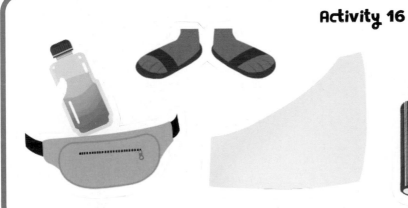

Activity 23

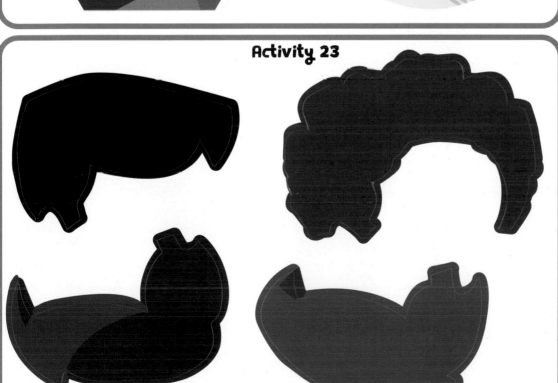

Activity 25

- ★ Jamarat
- ● Muzdalifah
- ✖ Mina
- ▮ Arafah
- ◼ Shave Hair
- ⬟ Sacrifice
- ⬣ Ihram
- ▶ Tawaf

Activity 18

- Muhammad
- Pebbles
- Black Stone
- Seven
- Big
- Milk
- Kabah

Activity 19

Activity 35

Activity 29

لَا إِلَٰهَ إِلَّا الله

اللهُ أَكْبَرُ اللهُ أَكْبَرُ

وَلِلّٰهِ الْحَمْدُ

اللهُ أَكْبَرُ اللهُ أَكْبَرُ اللهُ أَكْبَرُ

Activity 30

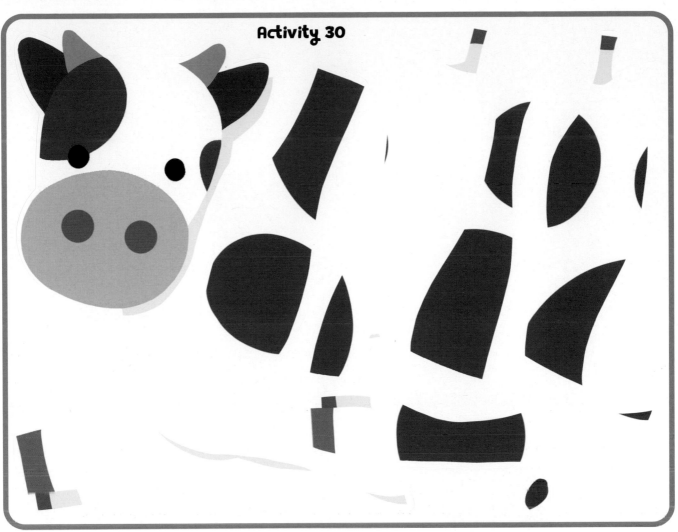

Activity 36

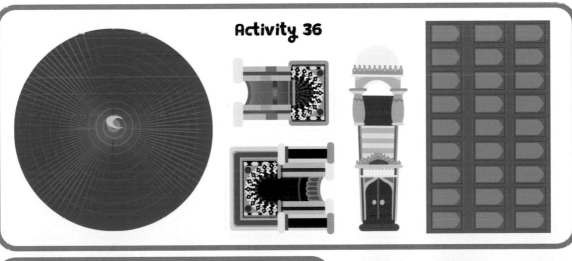

Activity 39

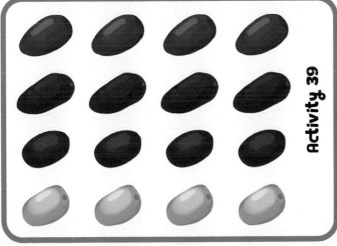

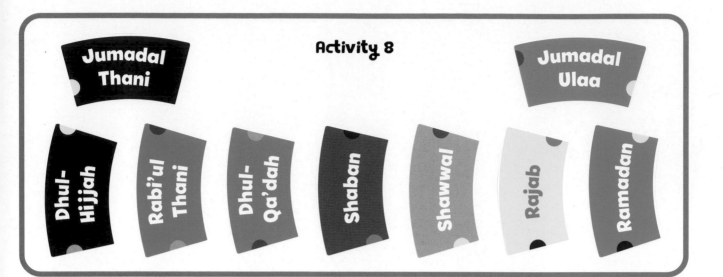

Activity 8

Jumadal Thani

Jumadal Ulaa

Dhul-Hijjah

Rabi'ul Thani

Dhul-Qa'dah

Shaban

Shawwal

Rajab

Ramadan

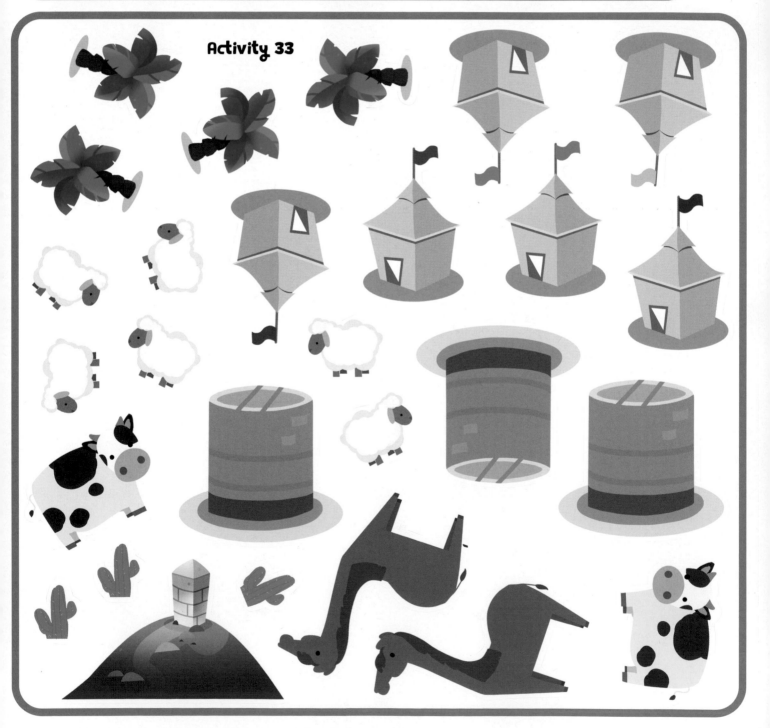

Activity 33

Activity 2

Makkah

Madinah

Jamarat

Mina

Miqat

Muzdalifah

Arafah

Hajj
& Umrah
★ **VISA** ★

Makkah

Activity 31

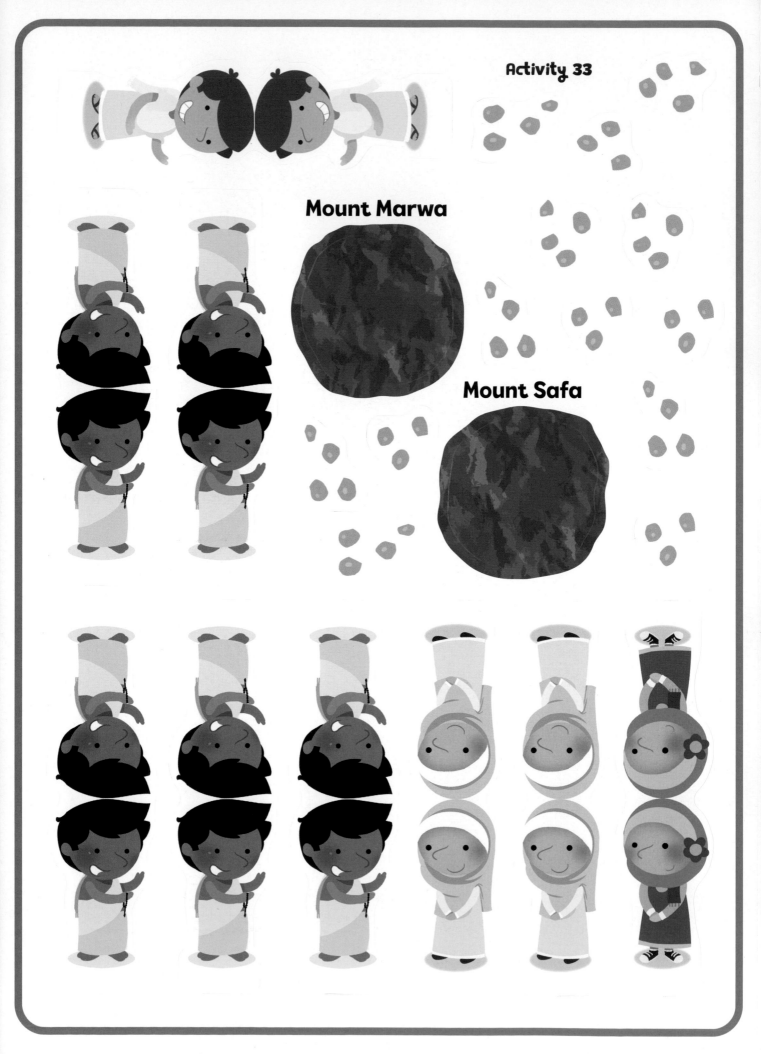

Mount Marwa

Mount Safa

Masjid al-Haram

Mina   Muzdalifah   Arafah

8th
Dhul-Hijjah
Mina

9th
Dhul-Hijjah
Arafah

10th
Dhul-Hijjah
Eid

11–13th
Dhul-Hijjah
Days of Tashriq

For instructions on how to use this pull-out, please refer to the Hajj Activity Book.

Learning Roots.com